Down the Baakens Underworld

incorporating Tracks and Baakens

BY

BRIAN WALTER

This edition first published by Botsotso in 2024
59 Natal St
Bellevue East
Johannesburg
botsotsopublishing@gmail.com
www.botsotso.org.za

ISBN:
print: 978-1-7-7649523-8
e-book: 978-1-9-9092268-8

In the text©Brian Walter

Acknowledgements

Tracks first published by Lovedale Press in 1999
Baakens first published by Lovedale Press in 2000

Front cover illustration (Baakens): Gill Morrissey
Back cover illustration: (Tracks): Hilary Graham

Editor: Allan Kolski Horwitz
Photographer: Basil Brady
Layout and design: Advance Graphics

Water Muse
For Cheryl

I hear the water run
in the shower, over

you; I hear your
essence of body,

shoulder, belly, bum.
I would see you but

some hangover of
conscience binds me

to this task. My pen
creeps reluctantly on,

shaping words which
in a clearer mind I

may be afraid to grasp.
But now you close the tap.

It is too late to come.

Contents

Water Muse	iii
Foreword	vi
Tracks	ix
Acknowledgements: Tracks, 1999	x
Nieu-Bethesda Cart	1
Windcraft	2
Workman	3
Swartkops	4
Lullaby: Alice, 1992	15
Dawn Whip	16
Domestic	18
African Night	20
Sihamba-nge-nyanga	21
Bushveld	25
Ingcuka	26
Lesotho Autumn	27
River	32
Back Home	33
Devotion	34
White-eyes	35
The Cuckoo and the Eastern Cape Quest	36
Seer	38
Familiar Chat	39
Footnotes	44
Nieu-Bethesda Way	46

Baakens — 57
Preface — 58
Dedication — 60
Voyeur — 61
Guiding Spirit — 62
On this Bank of Sand — 64
Lesson — 65
Antlion — 66
Echo — 67
Amphibian — 68
Frost, with a Shade of Keats — 69
Stepping Stones — 70
Charity — 71
Owl Crap — 72
Fairview Odyssey — 73
Gqeberha — 74
Touchstones — 75
Charon — 76
Flood — 78
Eating a Naartjie — 79
Direction — 80
Floods: 1968 — 82
Port Elizabeth — 86
Lea Place Guide — 90
The Guineafowl Trail — 92
The Hill — 104
Fort Frederick — 105
City Muse — 106
Albuca Longifolia — 110

Foreword

My first two collections – *Tracks* and *Baakens* – were written and published while I lived in Alice, or eDikeni (at the marsh [1]), on the banks of the Thyume River, and taught at the University of Fort Hare. I was honoured to be asked by the Reverend Bongani Ntisana to submit a collection (which became *Tracks*) to be considered for publication in honour of the 175th anniversary of Lovedale Press.

Thus, Lovedale led me into the world of publishing, and I shall always be grateful to the Press and the staff there, with some of whom I am still in contact. There are deserving campaigns to support this historic institution, and I am hopeful that the Press and its staff will continue to serve our literature.

In my mind, I can't separate these texts from their Lovedale origins, and it was with a sense of nostalgia that I asked the Press to release the books, that had once appeared separately, for republication in a different format. The reprinting was occasioned by a few considerations: starting with Baakens which I always felt was not yet "done", and which needed more editing.

This was only a niggle until the name of Port Elizabeth was changed to Gqeberha, the old Khoi word for the Baakens. The etymology I first found was that the word meant "in the valley" or "valley river", [2] but I have heard other suggestions since, relating particularly to the riverine vegetation.

"Gqeberha" is the name of the Walmer Township, the subject of much debate when I was young as the Nationalists wished to bulldoze it down as they had done to other nearby areas. "Kabega" – an Anglicization of the same word – names

---

1   Raper, Peter E. (2004). *The New Dictionary of South African Place Names*. Johannesburg: Jonathan Ball.
2. Raper, Peter E. (2004)

a suburb near the source of the river. Thus, the word was in the air. However, the word "Gqeberha" did not appear in the first edition: it had fallen somewhat out of general use in relation to the valley. That changed with the city's name change, and the niggly editing I wanted to do became an imperative.

With *Tracks* I initially wished to do only a little editing. But the journeys in the opening and closing sequences seemed to tie in with the catabasis of *Baakens*. It seemed that they should be read together, and the idea of one book started growing on me. Working with Allan Kolski Horwitz, moreover, enabled a fresh look at the poems in each book, and he has helped me shape them, and made them easier on both eye and voice. I am grateful for his interest.

A reprint, however, brings up the issues of the recent name changes of local towns: in most cases I have hesitantly chosen to keep the older names. The text reflects on the past, and many of the troubles we face today were wrought in the past. The text is indeed a quest for kindness in the face of our history, one in which the very notion of forgiveness seems nebulous.

And so, I am most grateful to Lovedale Press for graciously releasing *Tracks* and *Baakens* and allowing me to reimagine them for this phase of their development.

Brian Walter
Gqeberha, 2024

Tracks

Acknowledgements: Tracks, 1999

Versions of some of these poems have appeared in New Contrast; some were written for the Caversham Poetry and Print Project with artist Hilary Graham, poet Cathal Lagan and master printer Malcolm Christian, at the Caversham Press, near Howick, Kwazulu-Natal. Poems from the resultant prints reproduced here are Swartkops (i); Sihamba-nge-nyanga (i, ii, iii & iv) and Bushveld. The Cuckoo and the Eastern Cape Quest was originally printed by Malcolm Christian as part of the same project. I am grateful to the other participants for inviting me to join this creative venture, and to the Fort Hare Research Committee for funding received for this work.

The last series of poems, Nieu-Bethesda Way, was part of an installation by artist Elaine Matthews in the !Xoe site-specific project in Nieu-Bethesda, organized by the Ibis Art Centre. The installation, conceived by Elaine Matthews, was called "Quest – a Journey into Sacred Space". It stood in an open, dry Karoo landscape dominated by a mountainous outcrop. This hill rose suggestively above a cleft formed by a seasonal watercourse in a lower feature.

The four final poems of Nieu-Bethesda Way were requested by Elaine Matthews as part of the installation, where they appeared on four mandorla shaped glass sheets, each facing one of the cardinal points. They were written in seed-like form to echo the shape of the glass sheets onto which they were painted, and the reader in the veld could approach the poems in any order. Participants could engage with the landscape through the lines of the poems, or, changing focus, read the poems against the backdrop of the landscape.

Other work has been encouraged by interchanges with colleagues Cathal Lagan, the late Norman Morrissey and the late Basil Somhlahlo, with whom I have printed some of these poems in informal publications for poetry readings.

Hilary Graham, who provided the image for the original cover, (now the back cover image), has also been an inspiration to work with.

Alice, 1999
Gqeberha, 2024

Nieu-Bethesda Cart

For Dylan – child of the new country

"Waa'n' toe nou?" he called, tugging his left
side donkey, guiding her towards the turn into town,
    for both animals, quite unbidden,
had chosen to take the *langpad* right to Graaff Reinet.

His *vrou* lunged a practised hand forward,
    taking from him the long, left rein, and kicked back,
her body's worth, as he slipped to the ground to stop the pair.
    And I was crouched there,
  on the roadside, at my boy's level, a raised hand
      forgotten in greeting.

The woman, tight reined, held all tussen right and left –
    human will against the animals –
  while he moved quick across to the left side beast,
  and firmly steered the determined pair.
Again, he softly mouthed, calm at the donkey's ear,
    "En waa'n' toe nou?"

Their boy, perched midway on the seat, turned to look at us,
 while the cart, swinging like a settling compass leftwards,
    cluttered off, mother at the reins,
  eyes ahead, hand raised in a farewell, unforgotten,
 so he must chase his *dorp*bound cart, and swing aboard.

And they draw away, stiff-backed against the jolts
    of their shared wooden bench,
  though their child turns to watch us still
  as the rumble thump of wheel and hoof float
    into the midday dust of the old Karoo.

    From this blend of *stof* and sound,
  the echo of the man's soft voice reaches us,
    yokes my boy to theirs:

"En nou," he asks, "en nou, waa'n' toe?"

Windcraft

The African wind wrote a poem in our garden,
　　　　much like Hardy, in fact:

　　all about the stinkwood tree
　　　　hugging up to our house,
　　　and safe in its fold,
　　holding winter leaves intact,

except that a young bold bough thrust a fist out
　　　　from under the eaves
　　into the teeth of that Cape winter wind,
　where it shook, bare, against the cold.

Workman

My father can make catches that work –
        locks and latches for any door,
weighted or sprung, and cleverly hidden
        to admit just those trusted with home-secrets.

He knows that a job is best done now, and well,
and must wonder at one who fiddles so,
        leaves work waiting,
        will drop all for friends and a beer.
        Yet he finds no fault:
he is kind and has patience to match.

But what does he make of one who winds words,
        and works at tapping away layers of sense,
      crafting poems as rough-edged as home-brew?

Who spends hours making his verse a catch.

Swartkops

> *i. Looking Back on a Walk with my Father*

With care I chose companion and route,
and we walked from the rod club across the flats
past the sewage works to where the flood plains
      lay hurt by pipeline and pumping station;

    for beneath the mud of Gqeberha's nether world,
        of Swartkops, New Brighton and Salt Lake,
        my verse crawls in its own dark shell,
        wafts in the smell of salt wind and riverweed,
        and shrieks in the cry of wader and gull.

These are the sedged flood flats of Fugard and Lena.

      Once, when I came here to watch birds,
some woman waded fifty yards, shin deep,
      to sell me prawns for bait:
            "Ek vang'ie vis'ie,"
    I said   then watched   as with muddy skirt held
      with her free hand to a woman-dark shank,
        she waded slowly to where on the far bank,
    she had left a silent companion to wait.

There was that in me that went with her,
as she looked back to see a birdwatcher stand
          like a fool, binoculars in hand.

These salt flats can fix those frail shapes of humanity
   we hold most dear: the salt-flesh of heart,
      an underfoot of mud, breath-lapped waters
   that in their tides wash everything apart…
         So, I stood empty on the sedge-field,
         my prying eye-piece blank in hand,
            with a vision of a woman ferrying my soul from me,
               wading to the dead land
            of her windswept Saturday afternoon.

Now let me confess that I wanted to walk here again
            to fish out that muse of a woman.

Of course, there's always some catch –
         I found no living verse on this pilgrimage.
         But her old memory shone like a barbel, river dark,
   as we walked from the rod club across the mud to the pipelines,
            then looked back over the flats,
         out beyond the power station to where men
               mine their barren salt works.

ii. Daughter of Memory

Now   I nose these old draughts of memory
to see if I can still smell that river-salt of the past.

I recall how once my brain crawled with the mudprawns
caught in the tin the bait-woman brought:
        dark shellfish, trapped in daylight,
      fated for an angler's thoughtless hook:
           groping feelers and legs
        moving my mind into pointlessness.

Still, I am out of my depth, trapped in an image,
where all must sway with the wading stride of that woman.

        There was a muddy whiff of grace,
        for her poor beauty carried me away
        from myself, to strive always to find
        the old, salted heart of all humankind.

  Yet I've seen little poetry in this world.

We creep in a circle, swayed by wants
beyond our own.
                If I could only sketch,
in true fond fullness, our empty lives,
or feel the heart that moved her leg,
or watch her leg shape into shank,
        then verse may well come home to me,
treading the mud into memes of memory.

iii. Fishing

Near the old bridge, steel girdered and single-laned,
which runs north with its railroad twin over the Swartkops
      out towards Coega and Grahamstown;
   near the old bridge, then, on the rocks
      where we clambered with prawn-tin and rod,
         a group of thin Xhosa boys
     played in their daily rags of poverty.

Greeting us, boys to boys, they tried
to bridge what language would divide;
     but we, too shy, kept firm eyes
on rod and bait till one young guy,
getting right down to it,   dropped
     his ragged pants to show his small
          dark prick.
    With our eyes kept on hook and bait,
      the gesture never did the trick;
    but I guess, basically, it was well meant,
    seeking somehow, perhaps, to waken
    in us some note of common humanity.

We sat still   my brother and I
     smiles awry   lacking bravado
while our new friends laughed lustily
     and the murky waters lay still
  with the nothingness of bait not taken.

iv. Islands

Across the wide mud flats   sedge grows lavishly
            semi-flooded at high-water;
     tidal lows expire wafts of exposed mud smell.

Here and there, tiny islets mound forth,
            like the first land from the seas.
  Dry bushes, small-limbed and tough,
        bring bud and leaf and berry in season,
  while low windblown shrubs, olive green and dark,
           live landlocked island lives,
and rodent paths, snaking through sparse dry sticks of grass,
         hide crawling little islanders.

Deep under the brush, I'd find the little skulls
of mouse and shrew –
            those tiny island mementos of death,
      imaging full worlds of life.
    But, here, too,
  I'd find the signs of a larger presence:
paraffin tin, wood, and a zinc windbreak –
      someone was coming back to sleep.

    I'd cast around: no-one near.

              So I'd creep off,
    my young mind jumbled as a pocket,
      full of the bones and things I'd found.

v. Grunters

Once we'd see ripples stir the river –
grunters, nose down, feeding on the high tide prawn flats,
beat the water white with balancing tails.

"If you'd but drop a line in there," you would say,
   "you'd get a fair catch bagged today."

But now the river is fished out   with a few languid lines
planted by the most determined;

                  and those few grunters
that graced our pan are but storylines
       hooking us home to our past
             where you baited for me my hook
             and cast.

vi. Persephone

It was at Swartkops where my brother
dropped silently from us into an underworld of darkness.

      We   left rapt in the ordinary daylight
could not think straight   for both being and body busy at childish play
    were drawn into an emptiness and sank away.

My mother first broke the spell   shrieking, panic-struck,
            till my father plunged
into dark depths   down   to pull the boy back to living land;
back up from the dead water hole into which he, at play in the shallows,
          stepped and fell.

He'd known   he later boldly said   he'd drown;
     for he,   most desperately,
  had trodden the fruitless waters of hell.

vii. Harpies

Wind-free seagulls,
     with spreads of black trimmed wings,
scream their back-of-throat squalls
so loudly above us,
     and seem so much a sudden part of things,
         that we lift to them our heads,
   and they, imaginatively, lend
  our eyes and thoughts, their wings.

And, with those lifting eyes, we see the low dark hills,
          zwartkoppen,
    that mark our wetland underworld.

Now the line that cuts from here, where we stand,
    out to St Croix – of the three, the biggest island –
  will cross the place where those men
    killed Goniwe and his friends;
  suffocated their pulse of soul,
    burnt every clue of personality,
  killing to prove the rule of race.

Turning around, we see divides lying traced
upon the old town hills.
            That's where South End once lay.
      That band is white city.
           That is black … between, the brown.

But the croaking seagulls call us back to our walk this day
      across the present flood plains,
      across this mudflat netherworld
      where all dead and living flit together,
      where all possibilities start
      in sludge, in prawn-dark
          germination.
Perhaps not all life waits to serve some selfish turn:
      and the gulls shriek like harpies
      to help us conserve old faults
        that we   picking through this mud
      may more carefully find a kinder way.

viii. Crustacean

Once or twice in the old days
you'd take a crab-trap, baited,
and fling it into the channel
we fished.
                     After we had waited
time enough, you hauled it in,
        hand over hand.
The tension of the rope would shut the sides,
        and trapped crabs emerged
                from the deep.

I never, then, liked crab flesh   remembering
    the scream of boiled-alive beast,
  watching river brown shell domesticate to pink.

                But I ate it, I think:
                and as I think,
        my memory crawls like a cancer,
a grim revenger, for screams recall the death that lies in our past:
        that vain quest for humanity that defeated us all;
            that sideslip from our true selves;
                that dance to find a life.

Memory crawls sideways, eyes on stalks,
        never suspecting conscience: the trap
   into which   float-dancing   it walks.

    ix. Tracks

Out near the railway tracks near the power station where –
        for the white side of town –
            electric generation would heat
coolant water before it eased back
        warmly into the riverway,
        we fished at a bend the suggestive waters.

Picnicking there, our family scattered:

        my father waited with tranquil rod,
my mother knitted near the food basket,
        hearing generations of gossip from our grandmother
        whose tongue ticked over other's lives and deeds
        in time to her patient daughter's quick knitting hands
while we, youngsters, fished and roved.

Once, caught away from the centre –
        our parents way across the track –
we saw the Redhouse bound steam train bearing down on us.

        My brothers hurrying back,
   left me scrambling up the stony bank,
            the train monstrously close,
        hissing towers of dark noise clacking at me.

    I backed off   caught on the wrong side:
   here the power station   then shack after powerless shack
            of the New Brighton township;
        beyond the surging weight of the clicking freight cars coming,
      all picnic   all pastoral and familiar.

That divide still cleaves my heart:
             and when the last truck pulls all silence back,
and the way clears   I want to step across the tracks,
          bringing from the rougher side the memory
    of poverty, of all that we've done:
             of shacks nailed miserably against corrugated cold
             knitting in my heart the frail threads
    of our human reach to find metaphor:

    fishing rod   knitting needle
          New Brighton   mother tongue
                shantytown and power.

Lullaby: Alice, 1992
> *For Michael*

Hush, the baby sleeps:

let not the tock, tock, tock
 of guns downtown
wake him, or the knock
 of the teargas canister.

While the politician speaks
and buildings tumble down,
 we make with prayer
  a nursery of care,

a bubble-haven time, to rock
 this infant we have sown
into the world that he will reap.

Dawn Whip

With dawn, a crack of sound
rent the sky, and you, my dear,
shot up in bed.
        And "Christ," you cried,
                "what's that?"

With a fear born from gunshots
which every other night tore
the dark into their dead shape,
    I peeped:
        and the open curtain
          showed a dawn scene, sky red
              over the eastern Amatholas,
         tossing cattle-horns in the road,
              and the mud-red backs,
       all herded the eye from this heavy hoofed,
           nose-misted, grunting bucolic mass
          up to the russet clouds.

And the homely crack of whips,
and herdsmen's Xhosa shouts,
set the scene for a mind-play,
       as laughing at our fear,
         I lay down to reassure you.

For, as those sounds eased away,
        I heard the ghost of a whip-crack,
           a call in the night,
      the busy sounds of beasts taken
          in old wars fought
      for Eastern Cape cattle and land,
           when no-one lost or won the day.

And now   in this gunshot-loud
   whipcrack that made us both start,
echoes of that drama play out;
       and we wake, dawn-misty, into our part.

Domestic
> *In the time of the Truth and Reconciliation Commission*

First overturning their cage,
the dogs killed the chickens.

    "I guess it's natural," you say.

But the dogs never ate them,
      killed them, probably at play,
   leaving snapped bodies spread-
eagled, twisted and set in death.

   "Who did this?" and my mere tone
sent them a-skulk to kennel
      with that loping dog-false dread.

And for the dogs   guilt hung
      thinly in the air   they eyed me
   their only accuser   without whom
they'd let their crazy tails scamper free:
      but now they watched my accusation,
        tapped restrained tails tentatively.
  Yet then   at night   with dog claws,
    they dug them up again;   brought
back those bantam chicks to light,
      brought back to light all their sin.

The stiffened bodies lay soil-soaked and stretched into death,
   eyes sunk to black   hanging entrails part crust,
        part ripened with putrefaction:
    she, we called Cleopatra, he, a bantam
    Chauntecleer, dead now;
    dead hieroglyphs in dumb appeal
    for some dignity in reburial.

"And who did this?"

                I turned on the dogs,
      who ran by rote
   into their sheltering boxes of guilt.

It was, I suppose, natural to dig
        up such sin.   Their noses led them
straight to where the buried birds
              lay dissolving in that damp dark well
     of death;   and so replayed
their past, rekindled their deed, relived all,
       unrepentant in the grave's rich smell.

And in   on itself   my anger broke.
      Dogs know nought of what I feel;
   nothing   nothing of heart's turmoil.

They so easily drop their guilt and try
their hopeful smiles on me;
        and question softly with their tails,
           awaiting that sign they know will come
when all sin can drop away   and a new canine
purity lollop unleashed about my waist,
          and paw my chest
                  with happy soil.

But still my heart
            seeks young Cleopatra
whose cage lies caught in outrageous emptiness,

and Chauntecleer   whose chittering chicken voice
           was killed in his throat.

African Night

"Look," says the night   stepping over the hills
   with the moon full in her hands,

      "I've brought you this."

And she wears wild olive on her ankles,

and stars round her shoulders and breast;

and all the unfaithful violence she wrought
            is tucked to rest.

And so   I lift sad hands to her moon
         for she's brought back so pure
   and so peaceful a gift, so soon,
         that my war-ravaged heart
      that thinks it knows best,
            loves this Cleopatra-night,
            who's riggish but blessed.

Sihamba-nge-nyanga

i. She Goes out for Water

Kept close   shut behind dark walls
   in the women's round clay hut,
our young mother knelt
      by the dying crone.

The nurse rocked the infant girl,
      new from the womb.
The old woman cried with dying despair
   for water   fresh and quick from the stream.

It was noon.
The high sun dried the red earth clay

     and Sihamba-nge-nyanga –
        the moon-gentle mother –
  going for water,
          stepped into the glare
    of the forbidding day,

   unsheltered outside.

ii. She Walks by Moonlight

Years ago   it is said   at home,
   her beauty was unshaded love.
Her tread on sunlit soil struck stone-still
   herders and hunters and calabash girls.

Workwomen, watching her brown bodied grace,
could no longer till:
      she was too lovely, by far,
          for a labouring world.

      So shut-eyed indunas
      conspired to conceal her by day:
          she must wait for darkness,
      come out while toilers dream.

        Only then, she might walk;
    when moonlight mouths
      her darksome breasts;
    when moon-wide eyes
stare and stare:
      and hearts flap like night plovers,
and like plovers,
          circle and scream.

iii. She is One with the Water

And now   in noon heat,
a diederik cuckoo screeched, and noon high
cicadas sang: the still
      earth watched her walk
          to the living flow
where bush-willows sprang eternal green
against the russet of time.

She dipped into the stream;
      its living waters cleaved
        and pulled her down   deep down into the lulled life
of frogspawn and water mite
        to still brown depths, far from sight.

The sun sank in the dead west:
   dry earth turned in dark perplexity.
Then the moon walked into the sky
      – the nurse took the child to the muddy bank and
        sang till the moon-bright
          stream stirred alive
    and Sihamba-nge-nyanga
      rose rippling from the water
        to take the child mouth
   on a night chilled nipple.

   Alive   she brought her kindly stream
not to the dying   but quick to her daughter.

iv. The Water Rages and Earth Drinks

As the baby drank her moonlight milk
        the village men sought to force the mother
from her streambank back to her clay hut.

They crept   night hidden   to grab the water-dark
    woman and drag her home across dry veld:
but her river   enraged   overwhelmed the land
        lapping over pathway and kraal.

Quick floods drew the mother and suckling from rough men,
back to her pool.

   No: they must first offer an ox, atonement should be made
for both her noonday walk and their coarse sacrilege.

So when all saw ox blood seep down into the flesh-red soil,
      Sihamba-nge-nyanga stepped from dark waters –
          the lost woman found –
                  and brought her infant home.

But the frail crone's soul sank with the ox blood deep
      into Africa's living ground.

Indebted to the ntsomi tradition and the work of A.C. Jordan

Búshveld

For Basil Somhlahlo, poet, silenced in a Transkei prison

Unsure on easy paths,
        you scorned the cow-trod tracks of pastoralists
                and picked   instead
                the narrow duiker trails of the hunted
                where thorns of acacia
    like fingers rudely raised   would thrust
                and poke at your humanity.

        Your life was argument,
        your ground held only
                by the spoor you left.

  But now   in my memory
you are yourself a rooted thorn tree,
        a wag-'n-bietjie boom of wryness,
stopping all who hurry to meetings,
   agendas in their heads.

        And I think   one day
          when from my too settled ways,
        I scramble   terror-chased
        from rhinoceros spirits of conscience,

   yours will be the thorn tree
I clamber up   cutting flesh on points
   you have made
                to come to rest
        in the boughs of your uncertainty.

Ingcuka

It was a wonder when some years ago   a farmer shot
that brown hyena near Port Alfred;

      for hyenas, as all men knew,
were extinct on those lands.
        yet this loner had edged
          through miles of Karoo, down
            from Kalahari's timeless sands,
   through farmyard and fence wire,
               scorning all law in this settled pale;

and though shot dead,   that matted,
        low-slung beast still lopes
           through the dim outback
of my brain,
         slinking under the wires
      that order my thoughts,   tracking
    through Karoo dry streams,
         lurking in dreams   homing towards
           that settled place in my mind,

So even today   in Alice streets
          when young girls sing
       that *iingcuka* scare children
            and eat bread with blood,
   my hackles know the hyena
         is homing again:

   that forlorn shade of Africa,
             outlawed and killed,
ready to tread coasts of consciousness
      whenever she wills   and claim
as her land   the settled minds
               of awe-struck men.

Lesotho Autumn

    i. Sketch, 1996

Here, harvest has begun.

                      Drawn
by two oxen, carts follow field track
      and road tar,
           making slowly
their old way to the village miller
standing sketched in this memory:
      a white-dusted figure pouring
        maize into a flour-softened red mill.

Distanced off   the transporters talk;
      their oxen grazing in the washed sun
while the electric mill grinds seed to powder
            slowly between the stone-flat past
      and the moving metallic   now.

ii. Building

The new road to the Malutis angles
slowly up through fenceless fields,
twisting to climax in a hairpin bend
set high, where autumn ice stiffens
the seepage, and winds cut the crest.

Then down in the farming valleys,
the road slices deep through Lesotho,
     severs villages   snakes by
  those lovely old stone rondavels,

        all the while passing the new shacks
          of cardboard, zinc and wooden sheets,
            flimsy against the hungry cold,
superficial and ugly amongst
those assembled rocks,
     those older cairn-like huts rounded into shapely
homes by the warmth of human hands,
    built with the care of a craftful eye.

iii. Progress

The dam's immensity of wall curves
concretely into life. Already, though
far from finished, water is trapped,
banking up, waiting to be pumped
to another world's industrial heart.

I consider, inconsequentially, tiny fish
who have lost their shallow rills, and
can't think what to make of progress:
the flooded fields and huts and paths.

So, I'm glad we stopped along the way,
and broke simple icicles from frozen
streams, and sucked with our children
this humble fare; glad for the delicacy
water brings, if cold and fresh and pure.

iv. Harvest
For Puleng

That night
          ox carts still plied
      the new tarred road, lampless
   in the blind face of truck lights
and their mechanized tonnage that raced
down the lower reaches
       of the pass and seemed
to thread my nerves in
                low gear;
they plodded along wet tar, boxed in construction traffic,
    and leaned into fantastic curves.
              And then when the slow carts
          loomed quick ahead
from the nowhere of the dark,
      a sudden braking as the trucks swerved.

There we found a car upturned –
      smoking, wheels rolling in the crisp
          night air –
and an old frail woman
standing beside the urgent road,
      her cart high-piled with maize,
            shaking with dumbfounded guilt,
        whispering: the driver had to veer
            to avoid her   and skidding,
               crashed.

Busy men helped the injured through the shattered windows.

    "Balukile?" you asked them.

    "Yes, they are okay," though the shocked
    injured lay inert, staring into iced autumn air.

A male voice called from the dark,
        a curt and sudden: "Where's that cart?"

We kept quiet   allowed ourselves to drift apart
    going in the night back to our car   where we saw
        the cart-woman jittery and quiet
            clicking her two oxen on
        to get them going   and leaving the tar
for old field tracks   making a rickety
            slow escape.

Taking the dubious gift of the dark
   she   artless   trundled soft and guilt-laden
   away.

River
For Lindsay Pillay

For a while   there   we could not tell
what we saw.   A seal head split the sun slant river,
flashed photographic and was gone. We guessed,
unknowing: perhaps a cormorant, dark
   raven of the sea, hunted the river flats,

but then   in a light-burst   two otters humped
and   ducked, once   again   here and there:
   small leviathan   otherworldly
           in wetlands all their own.

And when they went to ground –
           the water
calming into a glass of afternoon glare –
    I longed to plunge into river depths,
   lift an amphibian face to the sun   be
    one   at one   home in the full flow of being,
   ducking dimensions:
         sun   water   ground   air.

Back Home

I have left behind the bushveld birds:
               bustard   plover   shrike,
      flycatcher and kite;

and left behind the waterfowl:
          dabchick and   yellowbill,
shelduck   coot   and teal;
      and birds of forest uplands:
             parrot   lourie   oriole;

to hear again and see
        familiar   less exotic birds of youth:

   the homely laughing dove,
      the turtle dove of faithfulness,
  and the chattering mossie,
      that scruffy bird of venery.

Devotion
For Ian

You have taken a natural interest
in birds of prey   and reverence
falcon   martial eagle   and harrier;

      and I am glad to see you grow
           into observance
                that I pray
will lead you on to other things,
   so that sometimes you will know
the shaded world of the white-eye,
        the home-call when a bulbul sings;

      and that you be visited   one day,
      while you till your ground,

           by watchful flycatchers –
  a blessing,
        always, to have around.

White-eyes

Outside my study window
        Catawba grapes ran wild.

        I built a pergola frame
        to shape and tame
        the creeping vine,
        just as   inside   I try
        to domesticate my chaos
        of flesh and mind.

And today   with the last bunches
        of late autumn hanging languid,
 Cape white-eyes flit into my shadowy ken,
        hanging on twig and tendril,
  plunging beaks into lascivious
                      grapes.

I normally think of white-eyes picking
      piecemeal   austere aphids
            from tecomaria and wild olive;

 but here, in a green shade of garden knowledge,
        I see the carnival that complements
        the shaping of my Lenten thoughts.

The Cuckoo and the Eastern Cape Quest

There's an oke come questing from the heart
of the old Eastern Cape, north to the mountains,
who's heard of a prophet and a vision that laps
our ox-shouldered hills.
                        He says he's cursed
by the piet-my-vrou cuckoo chanting of summer
and faithlessness,   and the diederik that haunts
in the heat of his noon-ghosted brain.

        "Daai vöels is…" he says with unresting eye,
            "die vals stem van ons land
          en die stem van 'n bitter geskiedenis".

And he is looking for something that stands beyond,
for a cool light that fixes the land to a meaning:
      something to guard our thoughts from ourselves.
He has come to believe that hills are the old bones of truth,
marrow fat with the shades of a kindness.

"Ek soek iets van'ie aarde," he says, *"wat ek kan glo.*
Something beyond, *of daarbo, maar van bene*
         en bloed en die land.
      En die berge," he says,
   "is die bene en die gees bly daarbinne."

"Deeply, *die liefde*," he says, "is rock-locked,
below where hills bristle their still-born rage.
    These mothers have watched this cradle of conflict.
        And history, they know, is the false piet-my-vrou
           who mocks at the bonds of both mother and child.
    History has made us the foundlings of time –
it's none of our making but all that we own."

Then he trekked away south,

        and the hills were full silent, still, and bone-bound:
       and the creaking wheels of his time
           caught and refrained
                the diederik sound.

Seer

On an autumn day in Africa,
you came from your mountain
to tell of a face you saw
in your almond tree. Nothing
you say could alarm me: I trust
your eyes and mind, ancestors
have been kind enough to call on you;
myths are making you their own.

When you left, I humbly plucked
                for my autumn vase
a living twig of wild olive,
the last sprig of almond from my tree,
and one bronze chrysanthemum, the first
this season.

Autumn: you see past foliage
        to the very word of tree.

Familiar Chat

    i. Shades of St Francis

Low beams of afternoon light shatter
      as the bird flaps
           across the workshop to slap
  and flutter against the glass.

There is no saint's hand to calm the creature –
      our age has tossed away
         such kindness.

I must steel heart and palm to catch the thing.
    Once free, it flies to the rooftop aerial
        and broadcasts all outrage.

Down tipping its ruffled chat wings
      my familiar garden shade scatters
in song those notes of fright

      that recount a fellowship lost.

ii. Minor Incident

Child hitchhikers – sympathetic,
   my feet brake before my mind can warn
that ours is an unkind age:
        predators pick up children
  or armed evil might well lie hidden
          behind this dry Eastern Cape shrub.
But children image such familiar thoughts –
    an own childhood lost –
         and already I have stopped.
With gears in neutral   the car rocks idling
on the road's hot verge   and two small girls run up
seeking relief from air that cracks under a fire-
              breath sun.

  Thin and dark   their legs work beneath
     little lady skirts.   They clutch to their chests
   excited parcels   till suddenly   still as sun-dead
insect shells   they stop   mouths rigorous with fear.

They find a smiling white man's face and flee –
       sudden smalling figures down the tar hot road,
  leaving me, my head on the steering-wheel
           of perplexity.

iii. Magnify

In the workshop   pouring over gear
and cog   at pains to sort out and repair,
   my father would say   that to understand
       a problem   magnify it:

              "Those cogs there,
           one a touch bigger than the other...
           to see how they will work   exaggerate
                   their difference:
           think the big one   really big;
               the small one   smaller still.

           then imagine that the smaller drives,
                   and see the large one slowly turn.
             or let the bigger be the driving wheel,
           and discover how the small one speeds".
That sorts out that.   But now my mind
         magnifies all of life's unkindly deeds.

            Difference sizes up.   A mere disdain
quickens into new mutiny. In fear
     of others I fear a new apartheid breeds:
          small notes of fright break into finales of hatred:
               inhumanity gets into gear:
            holocaust genocide again and again.

41

iv. Flight

Thoughts flap into glass   scared
   by a nothingness made real.

I walk here daily   watching leaves
inch from dry stems   watching trees
   I've planted   battle the drought.
      Now a dry uncaring wind bites
   to the bone   our collars are raised
      ineffectively.   Cold Cape gusts test
the feathers of the familiar chat
   flitting about these grounds.

I've planted this place   seeking
   something pastoral: this sparse garden is all I am.
I am conscience in it   weeding demons of thought,
   irrigating against the unkind aridity
that saps our souls.

 I grow mad,
till it seems the chat   shrugging its wings,
   curtseys to me.   I nod   smiling at its beauty,
youth   and hope –
   I   who husband this footprint of God.

But you know   this Eastern Cape winter
   is hard and dry. People out there
      have neither tap nor land nor job.

See   the chat flies off: from shrub
to roof   and away   wanting nothing from me.
  I have no right to plot
this world anew   and no faith
    that kindness will curtsey to the call.
I am neither priest   nor politician
 no people's poet budding profusely
   with words seasoning in magnificence.

Rooting dry sounds from this clay,
    inching out a verse that barely buds,
  I've hardly a voice at all.
Naked beneath their fig leaves of rhyme
these self-conscious words cower –
   seeds of light aglint in downcast eyes,
  hand in hand   they go.

Footnotes
For Cathal Lagan

   i.

We witness on the ground, a tiny miracle:
   a moving rosary of small white flowers
    strung out
 like living beads, nodding along.

We bend to see, and find ants:
    line upon line of ants
working tiny flower-heads, one
  by blesséd one back home.

I long to see their blossoms banked up under earth,
  soft in ant-love fecundity,
    ripening with the infinite care
   of gentle-soul ant gardeners
    in some heaven-drop world
      in an order so other than ours.

But I'll make do with our miracle –
   this living rosary of flowers.

ii.

Speaking of the soul, or of poetry   we'd pick
through mud   then trot off again, talking away:

and I'd cast out eyes for birds   otters   or leguaans
while rising like the ibises from those vlei-lands,
        your ideas bodied forth.
  And should some thought settle too soon
you'd shake it up   as you shake
      a stone from your running shoe,
  and cast it out again to the open lands,
          or to the listening skies.

But let us say we saw a meercat there:
      I'd point out the bestial tooth and claw
    and try to find for you some other creature
that might well satisfy its tiny hunting jaw,

      but you'd see only the parable   telling why
the living art of some delicate dikkop egg –
        motley amongst the veld stones –
could fool the hungry death
    that sharpens a meercat eye.

Nieu-Bethesda Way

The Call

She was such a sandy brown being –
every man's dream – whose buck
       -turned firm stance of leg would
       call your own old bones to strain up
       and trot along, anywhere,
          although
       those full round eyes, flicking as dark
       on white as a springbok flank, might
          fix you, stone-heart still:

"Meneer," she said, "meneer
    moet van u lewe 'n lang reis maak:
    en u rekenboek moet meneer ook saamvat,"
and her eyes seemed homespun and warm
as the wild honeybee,   *"en meneer*
    moet seker maak van u rekening".

And before I could ask who had sent
   the summons   she bent her full young form
in a turning bow   narrowed her soft old eyes,
   and   barefoot into dustveld   went.

Departure

When I told the spinner I'd got the call,
    she became tight about both mouth and brow,
        but gathered without undue delay the book
      and things she had for years prepared,
        so all was done   as was her usual way
with deliberate unknowingness,
for she knew how too great a certainty
    would pull my mind astray.

Ja   she knew how I should listen to her blood and soul,
        her womb and bones,
            the compass call of the out-there things:
      but like all her kind,
    I soon found my fateful mistress –
as my shade grew short in the noon Karoo,
    and my flesh crept closer to the shape of bone –
      treading   far out ahead
   of me   most sure upon the ground.

Token

The secretary bird, *serpentaire*,
became the token of our trip,

striding the Karoo, knees bent
pan-like, buck-like backwards,

plumes tossed dark to the living air,
crossing our path more than once

with straight-eyed aquiline lack of care.

The Spinner

I found her to be like that hourglass point
which the sands thin through:
       her sprite rising to the upper bowl,
       her flesh bodying down into
       that fulsome bottom half.
This I saw   as to pass our time   we played
       some game of words and images,
   of passing back and forth ideas while
the dice and the sands would spin.
       And I eyed her well when I felt
this mistress of my task had slipped
       her hand amongst my throws so she could win:
   this word picture woman
       whose flesh snaked down the age-worn
     glass of time   as her wild spirit rose.

Heatswept

Whenever I felt alone in heat and glare,
   I knew she stalked
     the mirage out there ahead
        while all about *karoobossies*
        hunched
          as tight as I   to threadbare ground.

I was become succulent by way
of being.   For as my daily flesh
burned away   I grew more skeletal-twig
     each goddamned day;
     and what linked each bone
        to each dry-lifed next
     was succulence of remembered sin.

And that kept me going   I think;
   such was the state I was in.
And each day I reckoned my strength,
and balanced my book. I'd grant I
sinned in such a case   and traded that
for the few next steps I took.

Each night spun a frosted moon through dark crisp skies;
        each dawn the sun mocked
     with a cold-heart grey   then stumbled
      to that fire-black noon of yesterday.

       "I swear this heat will kill,"
  I called.
          But from some sun-dark bat
   shape mirage horizons away,
her voice rolled me ever onwards:

       "Heat,"
I have told you,
     "will *not* do that".

Place

One morning   when the hills seemed
     all in the way   embarrassed   their feet
   on their toes   she stopped me.

         Then she left.

     I'd never have said that this
     was a place to end such a trip:
   a valley leading off called the heart-blood
         to flow along with a promise
           of water   or people   a town.

Now   in day's cool   I wanted to push on,
   but she had been dead adamant,
        and had gone to ground where a koppie rose
     pregnant with dawn above a declivity,
       moist against the birth of day.

There was no heat yet in the breaking sun.

        I spluttered then   for the spinner's jest
          caught up with me:
       it was cool indeed, here, in this source
        of my mortality.

Absence

His heart
"seemed full of little
bits of glass that hurt".

This dawn broke with a great
vacancy, ground into hurtful bits:
an emptiness of quagga and *trekbokke*,
of a hunter's small foot-trail so telling
that you could feel the absent bodiness
that had pressed each print into each careful form:

an emptiness of hearts once plucked like the string
of the gorah bow that drew this place, its hills
and all its dawn-dimmed stars, to one.

The tendon-spirit that curved that bow is broken,
and who of us can now ever really know that fat star
Canopus, *pronking* in the grey hollow dawn, who gave
the hunter his cunning arm and flick-sharp eye, and took
from him a fasted emptiness. The beauty of this broken
place can never be the same.

In all the heart of this place, small sharp chips, as of glass
crunched into grains, of dreams that humanly dreamt
themselves, lie broken; in this place dreams
that could feel the dark of springbok flanks
ripple upon kindred ribs: sacred hunter
of the dawn, story-teller, singer
of the rising day: dead, ground
down, hunted away by men
whose own hearts would break
up and draw apart; men who
never understood
the game.

Reason

Any place
is neither here
nor there: nothing means
anything, really. This is no
soul-space, or centre, and doesn't exactly sync
with either pole. It's not Africa, in any special sense: not
more so than any yard of continent beyond that farm fence
of Wilgerbosch. And no way will standing here looking north,
help anyone think of the human hurt of the dead in Rwanda,
of Angola's lifelong war, or make a viewer part of any African thing –
black, Boer, Khoi or bushman thing. There's no trip here, in or out,
and nothing asks who you are, or I, where you stand; nor does the dead
sand beneath us fossil up images of apartheid's wrong.

So much for this place. What matter if, somewhere
in a hilltop grave, lies a woman who once wrote:

"When that day comes, and I am strong,
I will hate everything that has power,
and help everything that is weak?" She
was a white woman, and she is gone.

Be real here, grounded. Best you
watch your own head: don't get bent,
messing with the stuff out there,
or the past here, where other minds
once peeped at waggons that also went –
as might seem reasonable to do –
about their own business, cutting
brand new tracks across
a place they thought
they knew
to be their vast
and empty, dead
Karoo.

Balance

Somewhere,
out beyond that hill,
snaking through the valley,
past the town, stands Aasvoëlkrantz,
rising like a god from the ground. Deadpan
idol, giving away nothing, it's packed its own memories,
and will do and say *fokkol*: its *aasvoël* soul has flapped away.

It is not dead, mind, but "like when the priests of Baal
cried aloud to their God", they found "Baal was gone a-hunting".
Now we come and pick about this dry ribcage of a godswold, and grow
fat on it, and, like vultures full of flesh, cannot rise from the kill.

It's easy to do business with the unseen of a place: those who shadowed back
when guns outshot their kindred of the footfall race, and snapped for them
the bowstring that drew them to the moving moon. But we plan and map.

With friendly phone numbers fixed in our heads, we quickly postcard
through the sights. No tight-knot string will draw us towards anything
we see, and the unseen lives unfelt. So let's go somewhere
out beyond that hill, and conceive of such a god: think
south, through the town, past Aasvoëlkrantz,
across Karoo and the Outeniqua, down
through surf and salt rock, leagues of sea,
to that clenched soul of Antarctica
that fixes this dry land we know,
this delicate fulcrum of our lives,
backpacked with leagues
of ice and snow.

Shape

To tread
"…the path to truth,
at every step you set your foot
down," she said, "on your own heart".

And here lies the heart: centre, for now, of all
you know. Underfoot, time has stoned the living
past into rock-boned pods; overhead, what we call
stars are thrown eternally apart from each other. Time,
which is nothing, in any real sense, is what we cling to.

As for gravity, hold it, now. It is time
to dream stories. The stars
are splints of shining glass that she threw
to the empty heavens, and then, when our sun lies
wounded on the westerly edge, and dark dies upon us,
we know she will collect her scatterlings,

and that, even as we face the night,
she sets off to catch those broken bits
of far-flung stars, to bear them home
in the old sackload of each trodden heart,
and that she will puzzle the bits, one
by broken one, and shape
them, with her darkblind care,
together, to redawn our dead
and waking sun.

Baakens

for Cathal Lagan

Preface

The mouth of the Baakens River marks the spot where Port Elizabeth grew as a seaport, and the river today still trickles into the harbour. The river derives its originally Dutch name from a long-gone beacon once planted near its mouth.

Old artworks and descriptions of the city indicate that the river was once a beautiful lagoon-like stretch of water, suitable for boating. However, industrial development soon encroached, and the river has been channelled, in its final stretches, into a spiritless gutter.

On one cliff side, overlooking both the bay and the river, is Fort Frederick, an early British stronghold. From this point, the viewer looks across the valley at South End, an old part of Port Elizabeth closely associated with the harbour and fishing activities, and once a racially mixed area. However, in the 1960s, its families were forcibly moved to racially divided "Group Areas", away from the harbour, and the intercultural, interreligious harmony of the area was thus destroyed by apartheid's Group Areas Act. The people were moved, and their homes bulldozed.

Beneath this more recent, still well remembered and recorded action, lies the displacement of the original Khoi communities by early farmers and the colonial authorities. The local Khoi languages have not survived this process, but the lost tongues echo in placenames, most pertinently here, Gqeberha, the Baakens valley and river, which has recently been expanded to replace the name Port Elizabeth.

Fairview, further along the river, was a farm which once spread across the valley, right up to the present Greenacres shopping mall near Cape Road where a racecourse was situated. This farm was later split up – on either side of the valley – into a northerly white residential area and a racially mixed area to the south, with the latter retaining the name 'Fairview'. This non-racial community was similarly destroyed by apartheid's Group Areas Act. As often happened with these processes, some families living there were torn apart when relatives were classified differently by Government officials. Emigration, rather than allowing families to be split along racial lines, was not uncommon.

The Baakens Valley forms a deep cleft that runs through the heart of the older parts of the city, both linking them and marking the apartheid differences that still affect the map of the modern Gqeberha.

A plan for a highway along the length of the valley was shelved after public opposition, and, instead, a valued walking trail has been established along the river course.

Alice, 2000
Gqeberha 2024

Dedication
For Ernest Frank Walter

*You first took us down,
walked and pointed;*

*you were godhead, wellhead,
all to me: but now*

*you step a darker valley,
checking out the place,*

*foregone, voorloper, faithful
to us all. There you go;*

*but from this height
too blesséd small to me.*

Voyeur

On the flat valley floor below,
there, there … a shy bird family
of red-necked spurfowl comes out
at tentative dawn while I look down
from the valley lip.

A mating pair and small dark chicks –
   as though beck   becking –
cautious and aware   come step by slow step
   from their world of shrub wilderness
   into that small slit of a glade.

I have a clear cliff-top view as they peck –
               dawn-shy ghosts,
     hesitant and alert – into fresh light.

And I recall seeing soft lovers come together once
        in this same wild opening.
My birding eye   taught to catch
   movement and form   leapt to the pair
   standing perennial in falling light –
her lost face   snuck between his arm and chest,
       his head down   inclined.

But the flowing simplicity of dark hair in the dusk-light,
        coy and careless,
   was the thing that urged me then to turn away,
   to leave them be:
for my heart – young and shy   hesitant –
   was not unalert to the natural snare
   of all loveliness down there,
   down there, and beckoning.

Guiding Spirit

    i. Traipse

The steps are still there today,
           solid and footworn, as they stood
      when you trod those weekday trips
      down from the church in South End
across the Baakens   and up to the old Bird Street campus.

I have never   but in this fiction   been on those stairs,
   so my tread goes a little gingerly down.

     And, since they razed old South End
to the ground, there's no true point
           to this casual valley-bound traipse:
      there is   in imagination alone,
      a strange step down   and a step down,
      till your tread   up from
    the past   rises in sound to meet me.

You   a stranger self   seem from another life,
   and seem to have been close to me.   But here,
     in this insubstantial frame of mind,
          you emerge outwards as I go
    some nether way.

     Different muscles work:
your thighs and calves strain upwards against gravity.
 For me   sinew   muscle, flesh
     break my descent.
We are different   but we linger
     here awhile on some rest-stop level.
   Your hand is firm-gripped and solid,
      your voice strangely eager,
         but really not unkind.

ii. Sermon

The story you tell –
        from a stranger, directly intimate –
                bewilders me.

"Once, oh, maybe about thirty years ago,
        one Eastertide, I preached on the mystery
        of Christ entombed: dead, as we may think it,
        but readying, yet also ready to rise,
        and – you know – already risen from the grave.

"I sought to portray a sage impatience
        – like an alert Ariel anxious to be
                spirited from his gripping tree.
There being that week a race,
   I conjured caged horses: pawing, pawing
        their passion for release.
   This analogy from some offhand part of me.

"Twenty-five years on, I turn some page,
and gracious   don't I unearth the root
        of the old Biblical word 'forgive',
        finding forgiving to be a letting go
                as of horses!
"The woman, taken in adultery,
        bursts her cage of accusers,
        high-necked and free to sin no more.
                Marvellous that it took me a life cycle
        to find this release from our poorer deeds."

Now: why did you stop   and make bold
to tell this thing to me?
                You strain off up.

        My steps slope down the fading stairs
   that, concrete, still tilt about my mind,
        dropping me always into the under valley
of lost forgiveness and beckoning sin.

On this Bank of Sand

In the shady clefts
of the old psyche,

I look back into the depths
of the Devil's Pool

with memories still as fate.
The unplumbed and dusky water

is somehow clear
under the tree shade.

The pool gathers mysteries
in the arms of her banks

while we stand
on the prosaic sand

watching the river
wait.

Lesson

The Devil's Pool did not lie
                in our part of the valley,
and we seldom stirred its shaded
            water, lying drowsy and still.

But our schoolchild class
            once trooped that way, sprightly,
     down on biology fieldwork;
and I knew more than most
    those paths leading off towards
    the Devil's place, its water
    hanging always dark with languid
    lily pads, and slow time to kill.

Specimens found by novice-
       keen naturalists were mounted
in glass jars: slow shaking
          stick insects, a soft ghost-
   step chameleon, some rare
fur-leaved insectivorous plants;
      tadpoles settled in containers
we half-filled with river sand,
    to be set up in the class aquarium
       to prove metamorphosis.

But in the broad classroom light,
our tadpoles disappeared   one by one,
    unexplained, until an idle viewer
shrieked: a sudden monster flashed
      from beneath our sand and took
    another froglet, backing it
   down into its earthy element:
                       dragonfly larva –
spring-trap from the Devil's Pool –
jerking from our fear-changed sight.

Antlion

If we children found the small sand traps
        that funnel into fine dry ground, we knew
we had come the way of our temptations

and we'd fall straight to it – we'd stimulate
        the beast, tickling with grass his funnel trap
so he'd flick and grasp at air. Or sometimes

we'd plunge a hand into earth to catch all
        in a fistful, then drain the sand, grain by grain,
to bring to light, in time, the insect dragon:

antlion larva, the neuropteran ghost.
        There's an image, lost somewhere in this dust,
of angels and hell or body and soul

and metamorphosis, some dry sand maelstrom
        of deceit. But I cannot pin the image down.
Words become their own trap, grains slithering

over each other, till we flinch, and grasp at faith;
        or till some subtle hand slips in to undermine
our world, shakes each word slowly off, to eye us

  coldly, hunched all insect in the palm of time.

Echo

From the cliff head, smalled by distance,
        I'd watch him chase his own dog volitions
        till he burst the underbrush at my feet,
like my own dog madness, jump and paw
            and sniff at home base, an echo
            of my own journey – then gone:
my untamed wire-haired terrier,
        in need always of a wash, crazy rover
    with whirlpool backside, his tail stub pulsing
        above his pouting, his proud, dog anus.

But I recall a moment of cliff-top calm
when the Baakens waters bent slant-
            beam sunset back up into my boy
    narcissus eyes. Some drifting child
        stopped, and asked with a still awe
        that echoed my own:
"Your dog, out at the edge like that, won't he fall?"

I throated a virgin manful laugh,
haughty even to the child in me. "He
won't, ever," was all my pride could
mouth.
        And I recall each heart-thump
        choke of that thin shadow of pride
    and loss, when my family found him down
in the street, stretching into his own stink
 of death.   Dead in that mad road he lived.

Amphibian

Terrapins in the river rise towards air-light;
   neck-stretched nostrils tip the surface-tension,
      as shell-flesh bodies float, arms out
     and angled, down into the brown depths.

Now, if all is quiet and still enough –
          and you don't crowd the pool –
in the heated soft of day, they'll creep ashore
   to sun their shells on the bank slopes,
      close always to their retreat.

But with too much movement,
     when the conscious world of suburbs
      comes cycling down, traipsing by,
they'll slide back into their other being below,
with tadpole and reed stem,
     into a quiet unreached by those
   who do not take still time and wait.

There. A speck noses the placid pool
and draws our own air down
     into their water where the Baakens stream
     gathers into a bed of unconscious dark;
     down into the shelled subliminal
   of an old reptile dream.

Frost, with a Shade of Keats

When I crept along the pine branch
about a storey up,   I had no poems
     in mind: maybe thought of Little John
        in a green world.

I watched the guys below, the older boys
coming with pellet guns, pointing along
the path my young brother had taken,
     when we saw them, taken fleet foot,
     while I took to the tree,
        and therein the difference.

One urged a quick move on –
     they could still *pluk* him good –
but my branches started slowly
     to stoop in that bending pine way;
  and I, at the ending of the bough,
with my body weight and crafty mind,
     gently rode the slippery green
unfolding foliage down to earth,
     to settle softly on the ground
  before their startled eyes.

And what their thoughts
     as they shot close-puffing pellets
     at my rabbiting back,
  I never – till perhaps in this telling –
     never paused to surmise.

Stepping Stones

You were not there then,
        so how do I find you now
guiding these thought-steps,
    directing footfall and mind-print?

I am crossing stepping stones,
my dog in tow,   and I see
the next step vacant that opens
a gap too wide to jump: some clown
    has taken out the last boulder,
        and unbridged our way.

There, the missing stone basks careless
upon the far, deliberate bank   and I
am caught out here, in midstream;
        and so   it is time for choice:
    retrace my steps   or muddy
a path through gloomy waters.

Oh, and I know what you are thinking
        about symbols here and everywhere,
as if this short childhood dilemma held some rock-
        solid meaning you could find.

Now, while I write the squelch
        of tackie-wet   and as I curse
the long-gone person who took
that last dry stone away   I put out
        of thought whatever you may mean
        by your tempting constancy of being,
    the guidance of your alluring voice.

Charity

Some suburban swimming pool –
    chlorinated into sterility –
      caught it: a terrapin, free-
forming in the crisp-tiled blue.

So it landed up at our place
for a night in the outside tub;
   our house   in old memory at least
   was always in some small way a zoo.

And I, who wanted to get at one
with the thing, tantalized it, holding
   fish chunks from our last supper
to feed it, and see what it would do,
      till its neck came creeping out,
   for all the world a reaching penis
that snapped, my offering grossly taken.

    Next day, I slipped it free
from trembling hands into a cleft
of the Baakens stream, for charity
had left my dabbling, tempting
      fingers shaken.

Owl Crap

Owl traces below the edge, we'd crawl out
to peer down from the brink, and read amongst the pellets
  brought up there, and amongst the shit-white marks,
    the inarticulate bones of fieldmouse and shrew –
wee creatures that'd gone their small progress
    through the guts of an absent nightbird.

But the forlorn memory those long-gone bones
  now bring is of the fledgling eagle owl
a few boys found flapping in the valley shades,
    and   unfeeling sods   ferried up home,
              till bewildered
    by what they'd done   they forsook the bird,
      dumping it with someone else –
        swapping out their guilt
        to usurp a kinder person's peace.

So, for a while there, the still life
   of an owl worried that suburban room.
In the quiescent dark of immobility
   it'd sudden in-the-ear click, plosive,
so that all who entered there would spin
round to find two yellow owl eyes unblink
   at them:
          and have the depth of valley,
       and the white-stoned krantz-nook
brought right home, and briefly catch
     their own guilt, all our complicity,
     in that unfazed, round-wild stare.

Fairview Odyssey

The old maps still picture the tale
of the vanished farm, Fairview;
    and how the Baakens River first threaded
        her way through its heart.

In our young time, though, we only knew
 that the name lived across the river valley
   where all the coloureds would stay,
     with a pocketful of otherwise whites.

There, we bought eggs from those
   who ran ducks and hens and guineafowl.
Chinese shops flecked the odd corner,
weaving homespun with their workaday.

Our side of the river was neatly knit
of new suburban names: Glen Hurd, Fern Glen
and Newton Park.   The valley was buffer zone
  and border, tacked between world and world.

And the story ends dead on the sandflats.
A ruined chimneystack shoulders the wind
   where its bricks lean into bricklessness.
Two palms pattern the once of a garden.

Threads are lost; that side lies stripped.
   They picked all orient and coloured out,
split blood knots, bleached the best land, and left
undone that rough and ready tapestry of home.

Gqeberha

Olden words will draw me still upstream
to Kuyga Flats where the old settler plans
map the unspoilt river source that seeped slow
        through grassveld.

Here, antelope, lark-life and korhaan
once quickened the pasturage of Khoi families
    who mouthed the far-off vowel-clicks
of the Outeniqua, and the closer Kragga Kamma;
      who lived against the backdrop of blue-grey hills
        amongst cowpat and seed grass.

Now Kuyga is a word drifted down,
    away in the salt-sea trades of spice and mine.
The place, both river-source and word-spring,
is Englished now, and tamed into Hunter's Retreat,
    the sportsman's waterhole for the gallants
    who shot out bushbuck and oribi;
  who reworked the land in their image
and named the farms Bushy Park, Fairview
          and Little Chelsea.

Touchstones

At the ending of our play, we would sit
      on our warm brick wall and watch the workers
  walk back home past our house.

      Different men –
some talked over shoulders to groups behind,
    some homed silently, heavy with the day –
they passed our house, then turned down, left,
    into the twilight of the dip and across the river,
      homing to Fairview.

But on Wednesdays and Saturdays, horses
    clattered by slowly after the races;
led by grooms from the old Fairview racecourse,
  home to stable, they tracked the workmen's route.
  Their sweated muscles, quivering and quick,
  reined in, restrained into impatient high steps,
    they'd snort and shake their heads,
  click and thud their hooves on the road stones.

Different. The implacable spirits of the way –
  they pass by, shodden: like the lost grace
of some old tongue's charging words
  confined, and dull-fettered, by context.

Charon
For Mike Snyman, the truer friend

The dark group came down the sloping dongas
      where a flood had torn the hillside red.

"Coloureds," my companion breathed,
eyes fixed. *"Skei.* They're going to *neuk*
   us because we are just two."

His keen antipathy caught me –
     there was no escape from view.

And they called across the wasted soil and rocks:

        "Kom speel,"
       "Wat's julle name?"
    "Wag net vir ons. Ons kom daa'n' toe".

My older mate, whose word was law,
   pulled me back by the sleeve, retreating.

"Julle's bang!" "Waa'n' toe hardloop julle? Ons wil net speel":
  thin cries drifting across the stream like lost
wraith voices
      upon our everyday breeze.

We weren't scared, my companion let them know:
we'd just go home to ask if we could stay out longer.

"Look, we'll even leave our socks here to show
that we'll come back".

And so, it was done:
off with our tackies and socks, and tackies back on;
and we, in a thrice, were gone, bared ankles
panting uphill, home from the valley wilds.

"But when will we go to get our socks?" I ask,
mother-worried and innocent.

"Don't be mad. We'll never go back. They are far too many!
They'll steal the socks.
But what other choice had we, to get away?"

Now old time has crossed me
to those kindred souls I once flew from.
I drift along the stream's far bank,
musing on a boyish text of dirty socks and broken troth.

Sad socks, forsaken.
I wonder whose small and anxious feet
they fitted next.

Flood

The old dip isn't yet overflowing,
   we said – our thoughts running into words.

      The rains take a bit of time
  to run down the declivities and runnels,
    the clay dongas cut in the erica veld,
over watsonia bulbs and into the slow reed-beds,
   then down into Gqeberha, the river-bottom
  place of the leguaan, till the stream overflows
    the old bridge, keeping cars from crossing.

And our thoughts ran with the water;
    our words – fluent with gravity – sank
  into new-wet mud, then overflowed
  into dongas cut some seasons ago;

  the poem of our earth absorbs the wet
       from stanza to stanza,
   and mere man in his motor car
     must wait   till words subside again.

Eating a Naartjie

Forget the apple   the pristine 'fruit of paradise'
        is so clearly the citrus
                that Botticelli's *Primavera* shows.

In nature's allegory, there, you'll see
        evergreen citrus leaves that signify
triumph over time.   Defying seasons,
            the trees have chaste white flowers
        alongside a crop gilt with orange.

Now I break the soft citrus skin
        and naartjie segments fall to hand
            with ease, as in the Golden Age,
    till you beguile my thoughts:

"Can't you give me just one *housie*?"

Your old South End language,
the child-talk of the streets,
            calls me to the old homes
      and the folk: the flotsam of people
        drifted in from both sea and land,
naturally blending cultures,
their gods laughing like neighbours –
            till leprous apartheid whiteness
        tore it all down, house by house.

I look at the naartjie segment,
    your sweet *housie*,   hand it to you –
           a moment's paradise,
        a brief taste of timelessness,
            a *housie* of peace
    in this hard world of men.

Direction

You seem more inspired than I
    when I drift sluggishly into the stream
of the river's rough mythology.

Once, they say, passing ships
   sailing the spice route   watered
       near its mouth. And – God save
them – some old souls made up
      a beacon on the wind-blown sands
to mark the shippers' water points
     – near where she opened fresh
       into the roll of the salt breakers.

And, so, the bay of the lagoons –
     da Lagoa – became mapped
in the minds of thirsty seafarers;
   and the Dutch word "Baakens",
     crept up the waters,
  hanging mistily over the new English
      town that now struck camp.

Words waded upstream, nudging
      the tongued wetlands of Gqeberha
into the tamed English of Kabega,
   till you cut back to the beginning:

*"Focus your thoughts on that beacon,
beckoning all words to its source".*

Yet I seek some other way,
    countering that that is *your* idea,
    which *your* words may better show:
that *I* don't wish to plot direction –
    would prefer, like the mists, to drift
    that way or this, upstream or down,
        wending with an eel's twists.

But there it is – your thoughts
    have led me where I would not go.

You set your mark and challenge
    at the mouth where salt seas and fresh
waters merge their telling ebb and flow.

Floods: 1968

i. Respect

Old water courses, ignored for years,
    tarred and paved down flat,
        awake to the scourging rains,
and stretching their spinal riverbanks,
are roused to a new rapidity.

In suburbs, slopes recall themselves
and tilt their reborn streams
into that mad silt-red turbulence of valley
       where quick waters bulge
and, heavy with strength, push
   to the sea;   their only respect
being for old elemental gravity.

ii. Remake

When the water assuages,
we go down to see what art
the drama has forged:
   scenes are changed,
and new worlds play upon our senses.

The green bank, Ophelia-lovely
in its deep water's dark, is no more,
   and mocking, new-fangled streams
dance through fresh river sand.

The heather-soft lift of our valley
is cut red-deep in a maze of dongas.
   Some new ironic play unfolds,
     and the eternal upstart stages
a rewrite of the script of yesterday.

iii. Chorus

Hah! You say that up in South End –
    where your visitors stayed trapped
    into hospitality by the broken roads –
the crowing word was given out
that the flood was God's own wrath
  brought down upon those lahnees
who kept the land so sacred to themselves:

wasn't it all ripped up, and washed away,
their beaches ruined, their bridges snapped?

iv. News

All down the flooded valley
the past is crumpled and awash,

or leans, undercut, with new
truths gauged into the earth.

The last wet word is naked,
headlined and bold in exposé.

Though soon the dusty sediment
is out of print and filed away.

v. Moral

The boys go out to hunt
   among the ancient headstones
of the old South End cemetery,
 and collect what raceless skulls
 have been brought up in the mud.
The city itself lies cut and cleaned
down to the bone. News these days
  is of nature's strength and doomed
attempts to change a watercourse:
    of how the babel pride of building
     has been pushed aside by water
          and flooded under.

Humility prays a while, then goes strangely out
       of fashion. Teams are trucked in
and plaster their wet new flesh over
    the carcase ribs of town
 and settle more firmly the houses
that the rivers didn't care enough
  to weave around.

Without much ceremony, the boys
 are made to go back and bury the skulls
     again, but wonder how a portent,
so profound, could be thus hushed
   aside and kept hidden underground.

Port Elizabeth

> *i. South End Childhood*
> *For Stan Eliot*

After a shift stoking a steam tug,
the father – on Sundays – played snooker
   at the railway bar in Strand Street;
shovel-hard hands chalked down, deft on cue.

The boy drank ginger-beer, collecting
bottle stoppers, small greenish balls of glass:
   he reeled in the scent of men
              and loud off-dutifulness.

Father and boy would walk up Jetty Street,
   rock up the hill in a South End tram,
then amble the last way home – catching
   neighbour smells of curry, of roast.

But orderly men want Sunday bars locked.
  No steam tugs are left to work the bay.
The father's hands are folded and docked.
South End and Jetty Street now washed away.

ii. Old Holy Places

"The cared-for character
   of the old stone churches,"
 your mother said,
    "is what I regret most.

"They tore them down and, instead,
gave us such ugly buildings
  to worship in: to marry, to bury,
    and take the Host."

And up in St Peter's ruins,
 we found the very font
where you were christened –
   cracked sheer across.

Grasping for a human faith,
as spirit spilt from your face,
 you asked, "Could people *want*
    to ruin this place?"

iii. Flavours

Waiting for you in today's "Late Night Grill" –
    honky place, up-market, on the Hill –
        I sipped bottled lychee juice …
  too sweet, perhaps, and watery from ice.

Still, it enticed me back to old South End:
boxes of lychees stacked among the season's fruit;
        veg out on pavements;
red roman and geelbek hung harbour-fresh;
    the rich siren-smell of spice.

Sipping lychee juice today, I knew my life had lacked
    flavour,   waiting for you.

iv. The Port

The men sold us red roman and elf,
   bargaining under the notices
which ban fish sales on the Old Jetty.
Seasoned trawlers rolled, roped alongside;
      unbright, beneath ageing great boards,
     sea water sulked.

The port's old salt soul   cut from all people
   by the emptying apartheid of order,
          and the harbour itself,
    lay Sunday afternoon dead.

   Yet these sea servers,
beyond time and race, sold –
 mocking from the ocean face
all pettiness of law –
red roman and elf,
spiced with forbiddenness,
      seasoned in a rebel recall.

Lea Place Guide

"Eight mixed marriages in Lea Place, those days."

South End survivors of forced removals –
 their long years of memory bundled up
  to overflowing –
   are back in a bus.

 "And the wherefores, or the whys,
  lie just there, with the mixed couples.
  Self-centred Nationalists, sensing gaps,
  made laws to thwart both love and progeny."

Now, the old residents chat and titter,
  tap the bus windows of recollection.

  Snippets of talk drift across the seats,
  like "sorrow" or "hurt" and "tragedy";
   while "never recovered" slips a moment;
and "lost livelihood" and "emigrated" slink
   like serpents into the season's cracks,
or sneak round the ripe smiles of kindly folk,

  who point out houses   remembering
the tennis player, an old teacher, some *regte skelm*,
   or a doctor –
  and relate what their children do;
  or where they were moved; or note the dead.

I married into a family who dwelt near here,
  whose neighbourhood was broken down.
Today I ride with them on the bus,
      disgraced by men who'd outlaw
        love and bulldoze homes.

  I have doubted what *mixed marriage* means,
  though now I feel across time for her hand.

The Guineafowl Trail

i. To Prospect Hill

So, we thought finally that we should plan
to do the real walk down the water course,
traversing town　　　and find the head-space
where you and I could see, and point, and talk.

From the Glen Hurd dip, we'd first tread
　　my young valley haunts:

　　　　after old Dodd's Farm,
　　　　　we'd brave the traffic of Target Kloof,
　　　　　　skirt the dog club, do the path through Settlers' Park,
　　and find ourselves near the Hindu temple
　at the skeleton foot of dead South End.

And from there, we'd cross the busy curve
of Brickmakers Kloof, and so work our way
　　　　behind the old bus sheds　where　together,
we would tread your steps – my virgin time –
　　　up to Gordon Terrace, and to the Hill
　　and Fort Frederick where this plot began.

ii. Hike

Though   ponderingly   we had packed
water bottles and notebooks for our walk,
        it went nothing as planned.
    We thought to bring together all reason,
every smell, feeling, rhythmic muscle pull,
    each symbol – though it never is like that.

The children   quite naturally   gave us
no occasion: random cyclists and what-not,
            kept us from our talk.

This is the everyday: our off-duty doctor
 was called away, cell phone in hand, to help
        a mother's infant come somewhat saucily
into our world: our careful myth was lost,
and pilgrimage became a traipse *ordinaire*.

Busily mundane   we missed the deep structure
 of story we sought   that was   nonetheless   there.

iii. Passed Away

My young valley's girth, approached this way,
curves back on itself like the small, pale ridge
of dead vertebrae in some dog's wayside carcase –
     the cradle once of such chest and gut of being.

The white bones of the cliffs tumble down
from the houses to our feet   fynbos noses
our morning air   reedbeds come into rustle
     with the ecstasy of breeze.

But the places there
     of some lad's dreams
         were barely worth this pause:
     once all my Africa, my everywhere.

iv. Water Nymph

Where the white cliff articulates round,
and river pools wait in stagnant black-green,
      a small sandbank   always shaded
           from the suns of north and west
      lives day and night
untouched by any but the slightest
           warmth of light.

And to stand here is to be drawn in,
inch depth down   to where the larvae
of mosquitoes hang from the tenuous water skin;
      or one-foot kick their lives into
      a wriggling metamorphosis.

Here   tangled water weeds drag the eye down
the darkening slopes of still water,
      right to the rock-foot.

  And I am glad of our companions,
for this is not a place for one too long alone:
      quietness of mind and idle thoughts
        lurk silent and unmoved.
  Two Egyptian geese emblem
    long immobility on pale cliff tops.

Here the water-mind ticks with silent
insect boatmen, or slides with water-spiders
  softly dimpling the light of surface –
  this still pond-head   knowing its own despair
  thinks itself deeper and slowly down.
    It is well that now you call me on:
      for in the darkness curls a child
        that time brings back to mind   and I tremble
  to be gone   and to whistle him out of there.

v. Time-walk

We have walked now   out
of my childhood ken   beyond

my pale of law and all my homebound
        gravity of youth.

This new place is still virgin to my step but fast
    becomes future   now   to that long past.

        And the lusty valley-space opens
           to my gaze   as I turn to you;

but you talk as one for whom all
        goings on are normal, everyday;

as if the shades whispering round
      don't beckon us on or point the way.

vi. Target Kloof

The valley flattens here   grassveld
briefly opens up   the houses creep
down to nudge and twist their gardens
into this rare wilderness;
                now, also,
      our crossroad mystery is solved,
for where we feared the highroad of traffic
          would block our slow body of walkers,
   we find   of course   the gloomy underbridge
              where the river flows.

Here the rumble from the fast life of the world above
rasps and sighs with passing speed.
The chill beneath of this sunless space
              boasts its stark old sex of graffiti
and brings the immediate dark breath of human shit.

Though warmth of day beckons to the other side,
   I pause   reminded that the road above
was where once I saw my death – but that an inch
of tyre skids just right, and somehow saves me.

       I should be dead, thrown body-shocked and wonder-drunk
in a bruised and broken motorcycle thump.
      But that was another life   another lane.

Now we shepherd kids out of our chosen underbed
onto a reed bank drenched in sun where the suburb threatens
        to slither down across our path.
      We push out from the underpass
      leaving to their lives those above
who hurry upon the highway of the world.

vii. Pisgah

You say the hill is Bruegelesque.

I've been but noting the passing aloes
   the fragrant low bushes   and succulents
     clinging to cliff-drop crevices.
                      No doubt,
your mythic eye has much longer sight
than mine. Each step   going up   pushes
back the path's white rocks till we summit
under a midday sky   where the others rest.

We look ahead along the promised path
through Settlers' Park   to the bend beyond
where the river mouth lies, just out of frame,
and where that beacon stood.

    Silently, I check you out.

You are in pensive mood   eagle-eye
firmly fixed ahead.

                "Perceptive bugger,
Bruegel," is finally what is said. "Like
his crucifixion: such an oddly small event
   among the busy crowds of everyday;
the whole blessèd show ready to be stolen
by that damned foregrounding of a crow."

   And I watch your sharp eyes cross
        the landscape below where our path slopes
  to the diverting world   more
     to you   than all my valleyscape and sky.

viii. Initiation

Once   a boy   I crept through dry reeds,
opening spaces   fighting through
to where the earth lay moist and shaded,
        the tall green reeds closing off the sky,

   till   –   like Acteon   like David
      looking and looking at Bathsheba –
I parted the stems to find a small quaint
 spread of water   and one black river duck.

   Alone   and I seeing the very mystery
of the place   and having looked my fill
    backed off as quietly as a secret needs
        to where from the sun-baked slopes,
I'd see again the prosaic brown bank of everyday reeds,
           hiding what I knew.

ix. Psychomachia

These black crakes treading softly across the surface growth,
    seem to have chicks secure in the sedge:
  there   a fledgling   tentative   toes the pads
      held shakily afloat by surface tension,
      while there the adult comes,
          insect in her bill.

But my thoughts drift off to Keats' lake
  its sedge as withered as a dry dream.
I consider death   what one knows of death:
and despair is a nestling in my blood,
      my adult self is bringing in its food,
        certain and resolute across the water.

I must think myself away to where –
  far off in a delta rich with rushes –
     the old Egyptians found paradise.
  On this southern bank   I find the great Nile
reflected in miniature here   across Africa:
  an ageless rich life   birds on water.
I try to nurse that long gone paradise
     in my thoughts   to get the sedge to grow
lush and strong   rooting deep against old grief;
to nest my peace in the cool shade of sedge-stalks,
my being in the shade of blue-purple blooms,
instructing my heart to live while yet living;

      bringing the sedge   the water and the crakes,
      the floating lily pads   into mind   to carry
      in the hieroglyph of this rush of poem-bed.

x. Settlers' Park

Tarred roads   and then the old turnstile
of Settlers' Park slips one so easily in.

Here   near that careful shape of lawn and river
    the distant thrum of the city is shaded
  and   beneath ghostly blue gum trees
      is softly overlaid by the clichéd
          hum of complacent bees.

  At the calm waterside,
        a Chinese painted quick-brush image
        of a settled dragonfly is briefly still.
        Stems of roundleaf waterlilies sound
the lightless quiet of depth.

        Here life is shaped,
                somehow foreign, as though art
had niggled nature into an obedience
and she must await a more sluttish time
        to bare herself into the untidiness of spring.

This parkland beauty seems strangely to be
a symbol of itself, a tidying up of history.
            It is restful here, but that is what,
    I suppose, such monumental places,
            in their crafted repose, are meant to be.

xi. Allegories

And here our group splits into two:

those who have walked enough   take
the kids to the carpark   but I   with you,
    push on   for we know what comes
when we leave the park and enter
              the older valley of a deeper shadow
  where the ruins of South End mark
    those plots where homely life was ripped
away and society unsettled – Dorasamy, Elliot,
Quanson, and our own Pillay –
       the shadow side of all that settled peace.

And we mark, just before we cross
       Brickmakers Kloof's busy roadway,
       the sorry irony of two sangomas
       who, the other day, set up camp just here;
not to stay,
   simply to do the Friar Lawrence thing,
   collecting herbs and tree-bark
in the crisp, dove-cool dews of morning;
     but the unsettled buzz of townsfolk
chased both doctors off to some place
    more secluded, more conventional.

Now a break in the cars gives us a gap
to skip across   then move on behind
the old bus-sheds where we find the foot
of our stairs marked by an old house
called *Nooitgedacht*.

                    I glance at you
for explanation   but you step quietly up,
musing on those old years when you left
the sacred heart of South End, to walk here.

I follow   sure there must be something
in these telling allegories of our everyday.

    xii. Aspiration

Of course, I knew of the steps there,
        had heard the family stories
    of how my uncle –
in the time he still played rugby,
      drawing his breath amongst us –
          for his exercise
would run them up and down;

            but I had never before wandered up
    that steep way – we drive too much
past everything these latter days.

As I begin to mount them, each slow foot with you,
    my eyes are maiden with vision
and cast on known vistas   angles that are new.

    Our breath warms and draws heavily,
but you are lost in an ecstasy of *déjà vu*
    in this return   climbing memory;
while for me   new things   once vague in mind
      now shape concretely
  and old spirits rise   and reform
    the newfound and the olden times we share.

The Hill

We remember   as we emerge
onto the pavements of the Hill
grey with clouds in off the sea,
      that it is a Saturday   personified
by that furtive guy   gin bottle
  in hand   whom the wind taunts
  and of whom you wryly say:

"Nothing another person sent him out to do
would ever make such an earnest hurry of his legs
    as those absorbed directed strides
        home from his bottle store."

We can tell we are amongst the living now –
    dead faces locked into motor cars,
       oblivious to cityscape,
grey sea and the still, toiling sky
    as white horses on the far-off bay
come in slow   almost motionless.

"I'd like an honest traveller's beer just now," you say.

  Still we keep straight along our route
    and end what we set out to do
      though – and I could not say
  this then to you – I must rein in
  half a mind that strays after him.

Fort Frederick

Finally, it is a lonely thing looking down upon a view,
    gathering the visionary threads
  that I need somehow to share with you.

I look around; you are a smalling figure hunched
      against the breeze on the wall of old stone
that makes this fort, looking across the ancient valley
    at the dead neatness of the new South End,
    as if there were some lost thing you sought.

The river is channelled there below into concrete guttering.
    Its mouth barely flows into the still harbour.
  The lagoon has lapsed into land and roadway.
          The beacon is dead.
The bay waters rock the trawlers out beyond the breakwater
    as I draw my thin dream closer
            against the salted wind.

    That you are a smalling piece of it,
    a brushstroke figure upon the stones –
    valley-crest, cityscape, background sea –
  makes this telling you so much the harder.

City Muse

In the dull of afternoon   we have risen
amongst old houses and flats
   where sports-keen voices from afar
have lured the spiritless into brutal inaction
   before radios and TV sets.

Lost purpose buzzes softly on
        and against the west-warm window glass;
the windblown sun is nothing like any human eye:
      no similes dare
   suggest themselves.

          The world is stale of art
and high-flown fancy wafts away
   across the scudding sky.   There's a race today,
and somewhere men live by bets. Uncaged,
      horses run through their quick moment
        then are led by stable hands back
to the taut nothing of their everyday.
      The commentary rides the afternoon air.

Inside the body   an illness of despair rises,
      dead with all that is   was   and all that
     the passing sun slowly unfolds
        in steps of shade   or weak slanted light.

Sorrow soaks through the unlit valley
of life and death's ancient compromise.
      Muscle and gut and soul, the heart
and breath of being, all fall back, give way
to the pale cliff-side impotence of bone –
      the Golgotha of spirit where wordless winds
        cut up from the sea-grey water.

 She appeared amongst the shapes of the city-sounds:
Buffelsfontein, South Union Street, Prospect Hill.
      I saw her walk the sad pavement of Highfield Road,
full innocent of my lost and dark love-stare.

      Dun of lovely skin, black her hair,
eyes no way like the sun, more than part woman,
      yet one brief part still child,
she trod the dull cement of Schauderville,
in those longing days of old apartheid.

  Her grave is now where children play,
from Motherwell to New Brighton, out to Salt Lake,
child-sprite briefly in their eyes, until saucily they come
      out into the world of rock-loud taxis.
In Durban Road, sellers and crowds litter
    and laugh the pavements to life;
and her figure walks ever reflected in this humanity,
this Africa, this spine of flesh, this finger-feel of back groove,
      slant of rib, shoulder-dent of bone hollow, neck,
        the Africa-curl of hair.

I paint her off the streets into some valley-space of our own:
                but charity, kissed once to death
                        delivers us the daily struggle:
Bethelsdorp, van der Kemp, South End, Centenary Hall,
                        Mendi Road.
The map of city muses on its past:
            Old Cadles, Berry's Corner, Five Ways.
            The voyeur of the now looks down
            on what has been and what is
            distanced into life.   Fairview.

Now the Truth Commission commentary fills the radio.
I dread the images of terror on the screen.
                I paint still pictures of her,
            portraits in her cityscape:
        she is no longer of our wilder valley.
They ask who finally can forgive those lost spirits
that wander in their eternal shade of compromise.
And, in these times, thin certainty starts to body itself
into a shape more real, begins to tread down
                    the old sinners of the wayside.

And what the heart to set all people free and release
                    the poetic of the just?
            When once she was taken in adultery,
                the empty coat of pride hung limp
            upon an idle tree but still she held
            that she was made of truth.
                        And still
            I loved her, though I knew she lied.

And I, with her, by small tact, bared apart by too soft a part,
   she would slip her lies past me, and whisper that love,
   altering with each newfound fact, cannot be love;
             my subtle mistress trod fragile ground
     enough, with all the spirit of her human will.

I think back into the long shadowland of valley-space,
where bone-white cliffs rise against the silent water;
where the streams of truth find their very depth,
  and still work their ever way through the deceptive mud.

From the brink of the damned, the grey city looks down,
     its dread nymph rising as her sly,
            dark innocence of hair
              beckons me back through a metamorphosis
                    in the floods that mingle the past and now,
                to know her in stark dreams.

Albuca Longifolia

As this memory shapes – miles away and times
from the everyday glare of smells, sight and feel of the then
        that once made a passing moment real
    with politics, history, its own mythology –
        you have gone, and I don't know where.

Outside, now, in the garden grows a wild lily that I lifted,
        furtive, from an abundance
    that grew alongside the climbing stair:
an unbeautiful green, onion-like, no flower to speak of.

    And this is all that is left tangible
            from all that child's wordplay;
all that verbose adult walking: no bloom
    worth the bending, a flesh-heart of bulb,
with layer under layer of its only life,
        that I gesture at, and – as if I could dream a way
to spring the corm-wrapped past and let it go –
    offer for sad humanity, unclassified, to you.

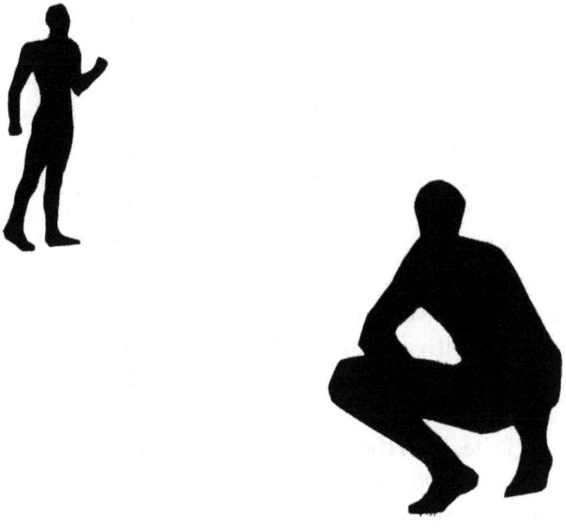

Brian Walter is an Eastern Cape poet who's been writing, publishing and facilitating poetry workshops for many years, mostly in Alice, where he taught in the English Department at the University of Fort Hare, and later back in his hometown, Gqeberha.

He established the Bay Creative Writing Development Project (BCWDP) in 2011 – a project of the non-profit Southern Africa Development, Research and Training Institute (SADRAT). BCWDP facilitates poetry workshops, and the resultant poetry collections of the Helenvale Poets and the Salt Lake Poets. He has edited or co-edited over twenty books published through the project.

These groups have recently been joined by the Gamtoos Valley Poets, associated with the Sarah Bartmann Centre of Remembrance Exhibition Project.

His own books include Groundwork: An Introduction to Reading and Writing about Poetry (1997), which he wrote with Felicity Wood, as well as texts for schools. His poetry collections are Tracks (Lovedale, 1999), Baakens (Lovedale, 2000), Mousebirds (Seaberg, 2008), Otherwise and Other Poems (Echoing Green Press, 2014), Poems Packed for Travel (Poetree, 2016) and Allegories of the Everyday (Dryad Press, 2019). Walter works with the Ecca group of poets, originally founded with colleagues at the University of Fort Hare in the late eighties. This group has also published over twenty collections (see eccapoets.blogspot.com).

He has won the 1999 Thomas Pringle Award for poetry published in journals and the 2000 Ingrid Jonker Prize for Tracks, as well as National and Provincial awards.